ultra sports

the ironman triathlon

by Bill Scheppler

the rosen publishing group's
rosen
central

Blue

Published in 2002 by The Rosen Publishing Group, Inc.
29 East 21st Street, New York, NY 10010

First Edition

Library of Congress Cataloging-in-Publication Data

Scheppler, Bill.
The ironman triathlon / by Bill Scheppler.— 1st ed.
p. cm. — (Ultra sports)
Includes bibliographical references and index.
Summary: Describes the triathlon, a combination of distance swimming, cycling, and running, frequently in exotic locations.
ISBN 0-8239-3556-6 (lib. bdg.)
1. Triathlon—Juvenile literature. 2. Triathlon—Training—Juvenile literature. [1. Triathlon.]
I. Title. II. Series.
GV1060.73 .S34 2002
796.42'57—dc21

2001003705

Manufactured in the United States of America

Contents

Introduction:
The Making of an Ironman

Larré has always been a physically active person. She bikes for recreation; she has both taken and taught step aerobic classes. She's a pretty good tennis player, too—Larré earned a scholarship to play tennis at Cal Poly (California Polytechnic Institute), San Luis Obispo. Larré enjoys her day job as a print production specialist for an interactive

A triathlon is composed of three events: swimming, biking, and running.

entertainment company. She works in a creative environment with a fun group of coworkers. She exercises in her company's fitness center and sometimes leads spinning workouts.

Larré is also an Ironman triathlete. At first glance, Larré appears to be mortal. In fact, at second and third glances, it's still difficult to believe the superhuman feats Larré has displayed on the Ironman course, but they are real.

Nine years ago, Larré became a triathlete. Along with some friends, Larré thought it would be fun to enter a local triathlon near her college campus. Larré and her friends didn't know much about training, but they knew the race distances (.5-mile swim, 16-mile bike ride, 3.1-mile run). They were confident that they would be able to complete those distances by race day.

It took every ounce of strength and determination she possessed, but Larré finished the race, and when she did, she felt on top of the world—and about as exhausted as she had ever been in her life! But Larré and her friends were right; training for and competing in a triathlon was a lot of fun. After a period of recovery, they entered their second triathlon.

With one race under her belt and an improved training program, Larré felt confident that she should continue to compete. Her second triathlon was the first to feature an open-water (rather than a pool) swim, but almost as soon as she started her stroke, Larré began to feel the effects of hypothermia. Her body became weak and cold, and fatigue set in immediately. Armed with an iron will, Larré completed the swim leg of the competition using side and back strokes and resting on the lifeguard's surfboards positioned along the course.

Clearly, this was not a good experience for Larré, so she quit triathlon racing in favor of running and cycling duathlons (two-event races). Eventually, a roommate who was a swimmer in high school convinced Larré to get back in the water. Soon thereafter, Larré entered and completed a triathlon that included an open-water swim.

Larré continued to increase her training and enter longer-distance triathlons until she developed the endurance to compete at the Ironman level. She entered her first Ironman seven years after her first triathlon. Today, Larré competes in two Ironman triathlons each year (with a personal best finishing time of 11 hours, 40 minutes).

Larré is a regular person who happens to have an extraordinary hobby. She believes the greatest benefit of the triathlon is learning about yourself—no matter how well you prepare, you never know what race day will bring. Larré enjoys the social aspect of triathlon training and the sense of community she feels at the events. Her story is a shining example for anyone who has ever dreamed of becoming an Ironman triathlete.

The History of the Ironman Triathlon

Gordon Haller did it first. Julie Moss did it in perhaps the most dramatic fashion, falling to the ground in exhaustion and crawling across the finish line on her hands and knees. A remarkable desire burns in the bellies of some rare human beings. It's the desire to confront the limitations of body and mind and, once there, to break through those limits and experience what lies on the other side.

In 1978, an athletic event was established that closely defined these limits. Every year, thousands of amateur athletes participate for the chance to test their mettle. They hope to complete the course. This event is the Ironman

triathlon, a multisport endurance contest that combines a 2.4-mile open-water swim with a 112-mile bike ride and a full 26.2-mile marathon. That adds up to 140.6 miles, which participants must complete in no more than seventeen hours.

The concept of the Ironman race developed as a result of a debate between a few friends. They were trying to decide which sport was the most challenging. They put the concept into practice. Almost immediately, it struck a chord with men and women around the globe, athletes and nonathletes alike. Today, triathlon is a growing sport with a rich history and a promising future. In this chapter, we'll explore the history of the Ironman triathlon and how it grew from a single race to an international network of official events.

The World's Most Fit Athletes

Not every triathlon is an Ironman, but the first official one—the annual Ironman world championship in Kona, Hawaii—was and still remains the sport's top event. The seeds of the Ironman were sown in 1978 at an awards ceremony following a running race in Hawaii. A group of race competitors discussed who was most fit: runners, swimmers, those who combined the two, or some other breed. During this debate, John Collins, a navy commander, suggested creating a new type of sporting event. From this event, the best athletes would emerge and settle the argument once and for all.

Commander Collins went on to propose combining three existing races—the 2.4-mile Waikiki Roughwater Swim; the 112-mile Around Oahu Bike Ride; and the Honolulu Marathon, a

The original Ironman Triathlon still takes place in Kona, Hawaii.

regulation 26.2-mile running race—to create the new event. The races would be run in succession. "Whoever finishes first," proclaimed Collins, "we'll call the Ironman."

And so the first Ironman triathlon was established. On the morning of February 18, 1978, fifteen men gathered on the shores of Waikiki to compete in the king of endurance races. Remarkably, twelve of the participants finished the race, led by the world's first Ironman, Gordon Haller, who completed the course in 11 hours, 46 minutes, and 58 seconds. Word about the Ironman spread far and wide. The event quickly became an annual destination for ultrasport athletes, determined to push their bodies to the highest level.

Ironman Evolution

Fifty people signed up to compete in the second Ironman event, and in 1980—fuelled by international media attention—that number more than doubled to 108. *Sports Illustrated* was the first major magazine to cover the Ironman. In 1979, Barry McDermott, a staff writer, was on the island of Oahu to cover a golf tournament. He learned of a crazy endurance race taking place in Waikiki and decided to check it out.

Recognizing that the story of this amazing race would interest readers, *Sports Illustrated* published McDermott's ten-page feature story. Because of the article, interest in the Ironman grew even more. The following year, ABC set up shop on Waikiki to broadcast the event on *Wide World of Sports*. A worldwide audience, including countless triathletes, tuned in.

Over the years, the event has grown, and so too have the rules and regulations. In 1981, the race moved from Waikiki to Kona on the Big Island of Hawaii. Race organizers did this in order to avoid the traffic hazards of Honolulu. The move provided an unexpected

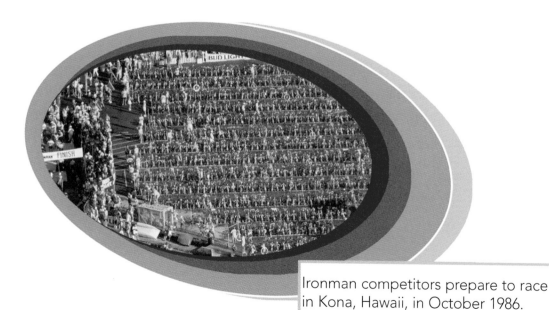

Ironman competitors prepare to race in Kona, Hawaii, in October 1986.

Isuzu Ironman USA

In response to the popularity of the Ironman race in Hawaii, a second Ironman was established. The Isuzu Ironman USA takes place every year in Lake Placid, New York. A tiny village with 3,000 residents, Lake Placid has also played host to a pair of Winter Olympic Games (1932 and 1980) and a number of other international competitions.

plus. Athletes now competed alongside the barren lava fields of Kona, which added an element of drama and beauty to the Ironman event.

In 1982, another significant change took place. Organizers moved the race date from February to October. This enabled athletes to train for the event during the warm summer months. And in 1983, cutoff times—2 hours, 20 minutes to complete the swim, 10 hours to complete the swim/bike, and 17 hours to complete the entire race— were established to reduce the risk of nighttime hazards. Participants are provided with an ankle strap, which contains a computer chip that signals to timing mats placed along the race course. Race officials use this information to verify that participants stay on the designated course and beat the cutoff times. If a triathlete does not complete a segment of the race within the allotted time, he or she is disqualified and may not continue.

Nearly 1,500 triathletes compete in the Ironman event at Kona each year. The entire race is broadcast globally over the Internet. Athletes from all fifty states and more than fifty countries—as old as

Jim Ward (*left*), who won an Ironman world title when he was seventy-seven years old, prepares for the 1999 Ironman Florida Triathlon with two other senior competitors.

seventy-seven and as heavy as 300 pounds—have completed the grueling course. As participation grows, so does sponsorship, with the 2001 event boasting a total purse of $325,000 in prize money, including $70,000 each for the top male and female finishers.

Global Expansion

Although Ironman's roots are firmly grounded in American soil, its philosophy—the desire to test and exceed one's mental and physical limits—is truly global. Almost immediately following the first Ironman events, triathlons of varying distances began springing up around the world.

Just five years after the first Ironman, Sylviane Puntous of Canada crossed the finish line in 10 hours, 43 minutes, and 36 seconds, establishing the new women's course record. She also became the first non-American to win the Ironman world championship. Then, in 1984, just as many Eastern European countries were boycotting the twenty-third Olympic Games in Los Angeles, Vaclav Vitovec of Czechoslovakia became the first athlete from Eastern Europe to participate in Hawaii's Ironman World Championship.

Ironman races were held outside the United States for the first time in 1985, in countries such as New Zealand and Japan. Today, thanks in part to the formation of the World Triathlon Corporation (WTC), Ironman is a truly international affair. Dr. Jim Gills established the WTC in 1990 with the intention of furthering the sport of triathlon. In addition to increasing the amount of prize money for triathletes, the WTC launched the Ironman World Series, which combines all Ironman events (culminating with the World Championship) into a sanctioned season, enabling today's triathletes to build professional careers like other pro athletes. The Ironman World Series spans ten months and twenty-one races, including thirteen international events.

Although the race has remained largely intact over the past two decades, the hype has grown. Today, "Ironman" is everywhere. Timex sells no fewer than sixty varieties of Ironman watches. Foster Grant carries fifteen styles of Ironman sunglasses. Twinlab produces at least six different flavors of Ironman nutrition bars. Wherever you buy sporting goods, you're bound to find the Ironman brand.

What does it take to compete at the Ironman level? Of course, it requires a lot of training and hard work. But most of all, you need a burning desire to confront and break through the limitations of your body and mind.

So You Want to Be an Ironman

2

The Ironman triathlon was created to test the world's most fit athletes. Today, it is also a symbol of personal achievement for many everyday athletes. Whereas in the past, the ambitious weekend warrior dreamed of completing a marathon, today that person often dreams of completing an Ironman.

There are almost as many reasons for becoming a triathlete as there are triathletes. Some people get into triathlons because they want to get in shape. Others try the sport because they love competition—whether it's competition against the clock or fellow

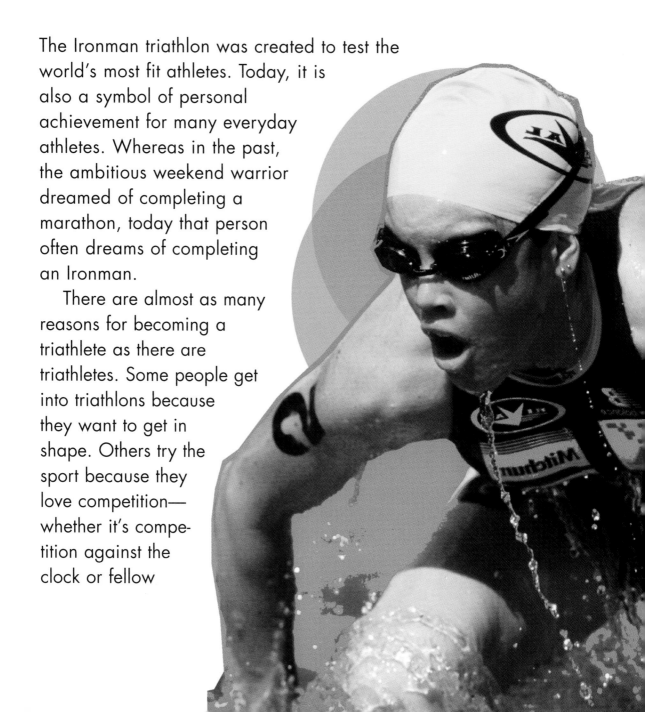

athletes, or just to push themselves to reach their personal best. Still others enjoy being active in the fresh air.

Although completing an Ironman race may seem like a huge undertaking, it is not impossible. It just takes time, dedication, and preparation. You can set and achieve several short-term goals as you work toward the Ironman. Also, there's plenty of help available to you along the way. In this chapter, we will look at what you need to get started.

Gear

The first thing you need to do is find the proper equipment. You're probably familiar with the gear necessary for swimming, biking, and running. When you watch triathletes on television, you may notice that they are using some equipment you've never seen before. Don't let this intimidate you.

Ironman pros spend thousands of dollars on specialized equipment, including custom-built bicycle aero bars—a handlebar attachment that extends forward, allowing the cyclist to lean forward and ride in a more aerodynamic "tucked" position—and wetsuits that help their bodies stay warm regardless of water temperature. But at this point, all you need are the basics.

The recommended gear for the swim portion of a triathlon is a pair of swimming goggles and a racing bathing suit. Goggles provide increased visibility underwater. They also protect your eyes against swimming-pool chemicals and the waving limbs of other swimmers. Because it clings to your body, a racing suit allows you to move faster through the water and helps prevent skin irritation.

Goggles and a swim cap are essential for the swimming portion of the triathlon.

You also need a bicycle. It does not have to be a top-of-the-line racing bike; in fact, it doesn't even have to be a road bike. Any bike—even a mountain bike—will do as long as it fits your body and has working brakes and gears. A helmet and at least one water bottle are essential items as well. You should never overlook safety on the triathlon course, whether you're protecting yourself from dehydration or the hard surface of the pavement.

The main requirement for the run is a pair of comfortable, durable athletic shoes. You'll also want a hat and a lightweight shirt to protect yourself from the sun and heat, but the shoes are key. If you can invest a little extra money at the beginning of your training, consider upgrading the quality of your shoes. Shoes designed specifically for distance running are lighter in weight than other athletic shoes. Also, their soles are more durable, meaning the shoes will last longer, and your legs will not tire as quickly.

Mini-Events and Local Organizations

Although you might spend a lot of time training alone, the sport of triathlon is actually quite social. Triathletes are a unique breed. It can be difficult for others to understand what it is like to train as an endurance or ultrasport athlete, especially if they do not share a desire to push physical limits. Because of this and due to the fact that long training hours leave little time for hanging out, triathletes tend to stick together. They provide each other with support and friendship.

As a result, triathlon clubs are sprouting up all over the world, especially in the United States. If you are lucky enough to have a club in your area, get involved. Your training will progress much more quickly if you surround yourself with experienced athletes who have answers to the questions you may be asking for the first time.

Many triathlon clubs run special programs for beginners. They hold training workshops and host mini-events for which novices can usually prepare in a matter of months. Mini-events are generally held in three standard distances: sprint, Olympic, and half Ironman.

A typical sprint race combines a .25-mile swim with a 13-mile bike ride and a 3.1-mile run. The Olympic distance, which is used for all non-Ironman international triathlons (including the Summer Olympic Games), involves a 1.5km (.93-mile) swim, 40km (24.6-mile) bike ride, and 10km (6.2-mile) run. And the half Ironman is exactly what you'd expect: 1.2-mile swim, 56-mile bike, and 13.1-mile run.

Many triathletes find it easier to train when surrounded by other athletes.

As you train for your first Ironman, work your way through the mini-event distances. As you compete in these races, note your progress and slowly build your endurance, strength, and speed accordingly. Many top Ironman athletes continue to compete in races of varying lengths throughout the year, as shorter races are an important part of their training routine.

Preparation

Preparation for Ironman training begins with determining your body's current state of fitness. You should also become very familiar with your maximum heart rate. Rather than focusing only on time or distance, triathletes gauge their workouts according to the rate at which their hearts beat during training at various levels of intensity. The reason for this is simple: If you constantly train at a low heart rate, you may develop endurance with little top-end speed, while training at a consistently high rate may impair your ability to recover completely. By monitoring your heart rate, you can set goals for training in multiple heart-rate zones and enjoy a more complete training program. To check your heart rate, press your index and middle finger against your radial artery, located on your inner wrist, directly below your thumb. Count the number of pulses you feel in a 30-second period of time then multiply that number by two. Each person's maximum heart rate is different, as is each resting pulse rate. A pulse rate of 72 beats per minute is considered normal. Training at different pulse rates helps develop overall endurance.

Day One

On day one of your training, perform the following exercises. They are designed to help you find your maximum heart rate for each sport. When crafting your training program, you can use this information to establish heart-rate zones based on percentages of your maximum heart rate. Using this method, you will develop a customized workout, tailored to your personal fitness level.

Swim: Two hundred meters using 100 percent effort. Immediately after finishing your swim, note your heart rate. This is your maximum heart rate for swimming.

Ride: Three miles using maximum energy, then check and record your heart rate. Your maximum heart rate for cycling is either this figure or the highest heart rate recorded during the ride.

Run: One lap around a standard 400-yard track as fast as you can. After completing the lap, wait five seconds, then note your heart rate. This is your maximum heart rate for running.

Focus

After you have figured out your maximum heart rate during each activity, take a day off to mentally prepare for triathlon training. You are about to radically alter your lifestyle. Think about your goals. What do you hope to achieve? What benefits do you expect to gain? When training becomes boring or difficult, focus on your answers to these questions.

You might also keep a journal during your training. Write down words of encouragement. Remind yourself how well you are doing and how strong you are growing. Imagine what it will feel like when you reach the finish line. Remembering why you chose to start training will help you remain dedicated to becoming an Ironman triathlete.

Competing in a triathlon is intense and exciting. In some ways, it is difficult to truly understand the experience until you actually do it. You may have competed in a swim event, run a 5km or 10km race, or completed a cycling race, but unless you've competed in two or more of these sports in the same race, you're in for a real surprise. Swimming before cycling can leave you with lungs that feel like sandbags. Cycling before a run can make your sneakers feel like a pair of ankle weights.

Sprint Triathlons

As a beginner triathlete, your first goal should be to complete a sprint triathlon. Sprint events are much shorter versions of Ironman events. Most experts agree that the average person who knows how to swim and ride a bike can prepare for a sprint race in just twelve weeks of focused workouts.

Training for a sprint race will give you valuable triathlon experience but demand less training time. Whether or not you've trained for other athletic events in the past, pay close attention to the training you do for your first triathlon. The type of training you do for a multisport race may be quite a bit different than the way you have prepared for other events in the past.

Sprint Distance Training Chart

This chart (created by Gale Bernhardt, author of *Training Plans for Multisport Athletes* and regular contributor to *Triathlete Magazine*) illustrates a typical training program for a beginning triathlete preparing to compete in a sprint event. It spans twelve weeks or roughly three months. The time of each workout is listed in minutes. As you can see, an average week consists of two swimming workouts. It also includes three biking workouts and three running workouts. Total training time per week falls between 3.5 and 7.5 hours.

Month One

Week	Sport	Mon	Tues	Wed	Thurs	Fri	Sat	Sun
One	Swim		30 min		30 min			
	Bike			60 min		30 min		
	Run				45 min		45 min	
Two	Swim		40 min		30 min			
	Bike			60 min		30 min		90 min
	Run		30 min		35 min		40 min	
Three	Swim		40 min		40 min			
	Bike			60 min		30 min		105 min
	Run		20 min		45 min		60 min	
Four	Swim		20 min		20 min			
	Bike			45 min				60 min
	Run				30 min		35 min	

Month Two

Week	Sport	Mon	Tues	Wed	Thurs	Fri	Sat	Sun
Five	Swim		30 min		35 min			
	Bike			60 min		30 min		70 min
	Run				45 min		50 min	
Six	Swim		40 min		40 min			
	Bike			60 min		30 min		90 min
	Run		20 min		40 min		60 min	
Seven	Swim		45 min		40 min			
	Bike			60 min		30 min		120 min
	Run		30 min		40 min		60 min	
Eight	Swim		20 min		20 min			
	Bike			45 min				60 min
	Run				30 min		35 min	

Month Three

Week	Sport	Mon	Tues	Wed	Thurs	Fri	Sat	Sun
Nine	Swim		35 min		30 min			
	Bike			60 min		45 min		60 min
	Run				45 min		30 min	30 min
Ten	Swim		40 min		40 min			
	Bike			60 min		45 min		90 min
	Run				40 min		60 min	20 min
Eleven	Swim		45 min		25 min		20 min	
	Bike			60 min		40 min	70 min	60 min
	Run		60 min		40 min		30 min	
Twelve	Swim		30 min					Race
	Bike						30 min	Race
	Run					30 min		Race

Training Goals

Use the training chart as a guide. It can help you determine which days to work out and for how long. In this particular training program, training intensity increases each week. The number one goal in weeks one to four is to focus on establishing good form and building endurance. Your main goal during weeks four to eight should be to make improvements in speed. And in weeks nine to twelve, the goal is to make sure you can complete the entire race without feeling exhausted.

Training Techniques

Triathletes also vary the way they work out, using a variety of techniques such as tempo, interval, endurance, and brick techniques. Mix up your workouts so that you never use the same training technique two days in a row. These training techniques also rely on the maximum heart information you determined during your first workout sessions. As you improve your physical conditioning, your maximum heart rate will increase. Repeat the heart rate exercise every four to six weeks. If your maximum heart rate goes

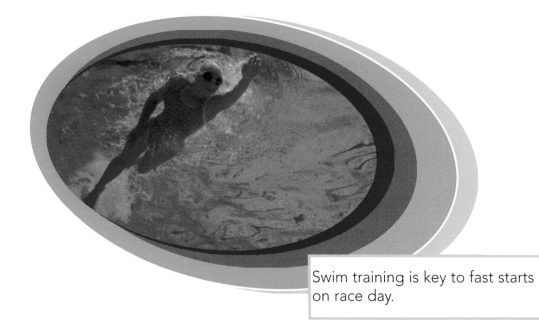

Swim training is key to fast starts on race day.

up, then use that as your basis and recalculate the percentages that appear in the following training technique sections.

Tempo

Tempo technique involves training while your heart beats at 80–90 percent of its maximum rate (the actual rate at which you should compete during the race). You should only cover 50–75 percent of the race distance. In the case of sprint training, this means swimming 225–337 yards, cycling 6.5–9.75 miles, or running 1.5–2.3 miles.

Interval

During interval workouts, your heart rate should remain at 90–100 percent of the maximum. This workout is at a faster pace and for shorter distances than an actual sprint race. Divide your swimming into six intervals of 75 yards, cycling into six intervals of 2 miles, and running into six .5-mile intervals. After completing an interval, rest for double the time you took to complete the interval before beginning the next one.

Endurance

This technique involves slow, long-distance workouts that are 150–200 percent of the race distance. You perform these workouts at a heart rate that is 60–70 percent of the maximum. Try swimming 675–900 yards, cycling 19.5–26 miles, and running 4.6–6.2 miles.

Bricks

This technique combines two workouts into one. A brick is made up of a tempo cycling workout followed immediately by a tempo

A triathlete fastens his helmet as he switches to biking during the 2001 Australian Triathlon Championship.

running workout. This training session will do two things: help you to work on the transition from the bike race to the run, and give you experience dealing with doing one activity right after another. The brick workout is an advanced technique that does not appear on the training chart until the third month. Notice the workouts stacked together in weeks nine to eleven. These are brick training days.

Use this workout plan and these techniques to help you complete your first sprint triathlon. After completing your first sprint, change your training program and focus on more advanced goals, such as improving your finish time, being competitive against other participants in your age group, or entering longer-distance races.

Nutrition

The leading cause of poor triathlon performance is not poor training or conditioning, but poor nutrition. Athletics and nutrition go hand-in-hand. Proper nutrition is especially important when it comes to endurance sports. Training for and competing in a triathlon takes a lot out of your body, so you'll have to get used to putting a lot into your body.

The nutritional and hydrational (food and fluid) demands of triathlon are more intense than those of single sport events. This means you will need to eat and drink more than you normally would. During a race, some triathletes are forced to reduce their pace or withdraw from a race altogether simply because they run out of energy. In this chapter, we'll provide some

Ironman triathletes eat carbohydrate-rich foods such as bananas to maintain energy.

general dietary information and outline a few nutritional guidelines for triathletes.

Eating for Performance

The foods we eat can be divided into three basic categories: carbohydrates (carbs), proteins, and fats. As your training progresses, your nutritional knowledge should also grow. You must also increase your understanding of how your body responds to various foods. There is plenty to learn, and the best

Muscle Cramps

When a muscle has been working hard or is overworked, it will sometimes involuntarily knot up or spasm. This can be very painful and can easily bring even the strongest athlete to his or her knees. Muscle cramps are most common after long training sessions or during/after races, especially if an athlete has been sweating a lot. Drinking plenty of fluids throughout training and during a race can help prevent cramps. If cramps do occur, gently stretch the distressed muscle.

way to find out is to explore a variety of resources and learn through well-informed trial and error.

Our bodies function by burning calories and converting them into energy. Even when we're at rest, our bodies burn calories at a low rate. While at rest, about 60 percent of the calories we burn are stored fat, while 35 percent are carbs and 5 percent are protein. As we become more active, our bodies burn more carbohydrates. During high-intensity workouts, bodies typically burn 95 percent carbs, 3 percent fat, and 2 percent protein.

Carbohydrates

Every gram of carbohydrate provides the body with four calories of potential energy, but our bodies can store only around 2,000 calories of carbohydrates in our muscles at any given time. This can pose a problem for triathletes. The multiple weekly training sessions burn such a high number of carbohydrates that it is difficult for their bodies to store all the carbohydrates they need. In order to maintain high energy levels, it is important to add carbohydrates lost during long workouts and races. Whole-grain bagels, pasta, and brown rice are excellent sources of complex carbohydrates, which break down slowly and fuel your system for an extended period of time. Foods that are high in sugar are also high in carbohydrates, but these are simple carbohydrates, which break down quickly and often end up stored in fat cells.

Protein

Like carbohydrates, protein contains four calories per gram. Only a very small amount of protein calories are burned as energy, and this amount shrinks as activity increases. Our bodies use protein calories much more efficiently. The body converts protein into amino acids. They in turn go to work repairing depleted muscle tissue. Because the body breaks down protein in this way, it is best to eat protein-rich foods after a race or workout rather than before. That way, protein calories will be in a better position to do their job. Meat, such as beef, poultry, and fish, is high in protein calories. Non-meat sources of protein include soy products, nuts, beans, eggs, and dairy products.

Fat

In today's society, fat gets a bad rap. If you simply pay attention to the media and advertising, you might think that any fat in your diet is a bad thing. This is not true. Saturated fats—mostly from animal fats—should be eaten in moderation. Unsaturated fats—from olive or canola oil—are needed for proper body nutrition. Of course, all fats should be eaten in moderation. A normal diet should not exceed 65 grams of fat in a single day.

As a triathlete, your carbohydrate and protein calories are important allies during and after a workout. What about when you're not training? As mentioned above, when at rest, 60 percent of the calories you burn are fat calories. This is to your advantage. It means you're not wasting your limited carbohydrate reserves, which you'll call upon for your next training session.

Although we're not discussing vitamins in this chapter, it's important to note that many vitamins are fat-soluble, which means your body uses fat to break them down into usable nutrients. A diet that is extremely low in fat could actually cause health problems, as your body may be unable to absorb the vitamins you need. Many excellent protein sources also contain a fair amount of fat. Cheese, whole milk, and even peanut butter contain significant fat calories, but ingested in moderation these calories will burn off rather than build up. If you're interested in cutting fat out of your diet, say no to things like fried foods and take it easy on the butter.

Ironman competitors need to stay hydrated during the race.

Fueling Up

Always begin your workout with a full tank of energy. This does not mean starting with a full stomach. A full tank means your carbohydrate reserves, stored in muscle cells, are high. You will have to do some experimentation with your body to find the perfect mix between a full tank and a full stomach. Generally speaking, try to ingest sixty to eighty grams of carbohydrates shortly before any workout. Bananas contain about thirty grams of carbohydrates; most energy bars have about forty. Check the nutritional information on your food labels for the carbohydrate makeup of specific items.

During long training sessions, be sure to consume additional calories as needed. For example, if your workout runs ninety minutes or longer, ingest about twenty grams of carbs every thirty minutes. You should eat these carbohydrates in as concentrated a form as possible so as not to fill your stomach. You can do this fairly easily with a few fig bars or half an energy bar.

Hydration

Staying properly hydrated (drinking enough fluids) is key. You should drink at least eight eight-ounce glasses of water every day to maintain your body's optimum hydration level. To make sure you have enough fluids in your system before a training session, consume sixteen ounces of water or sports drink about an hour before you begin. This gives your body enough time to process the fluids so you won't have to endure painful side aches.

Your body needs water constantly, even before you feel thirsty. During your workout, reach for your water bottle at regular intervals to stay a step ahead of dehydration. Your bike should have a water-bottle mount on the frame, in which you can carry your bottle. While on the run, you can either carry a bottle or purchase a belt designed to hold one or more water bottles. If you're swimming laps in a pool, just keep your bottle on the edge of the pool at the end of your lane and pause to drink when the time comes. With proper training and nutrition, you'll be ready for your first event.

5 Race Day

You've dedicated the past three months of your life to preparing for this day. You changed your eating habits, increased your physical endurance, and are more in tune with your body than ever before.

Your first triathlon is a huge event in your life. Although you may be nervous about conquering all the twists and turns of the course and the skill level of the competition, you know what you can do. You're confident that you have what it takes to complete the event.

Final Preparation

Your workouts should trail off dramatically in the final week before the event. Take advantage of this downtime to rest your body, build your carbohydrate reserves, and prepare mentally for the race.

Drink a lot of water a day or two before the race to reduce the risk of dehydration during the event. Just drinking a lot of water on the morning of race day or even the night before will not do the trick. Dehydration will result in muscle cramps, which can end your race several miles before you planned.

Before the Race

On race day, wake up early and be sure to eat a well-balanced meal two to three hours before the start of the triathlon. Ingest only foods that you've been eating during your training program. Race day is not the time to experiment with new foods.

Get to the course early—an hour before the race begins is not too soon. There is plenty to do before the race. First, set up your equipment in the transition, or changing, areas. When you get out of the water, the last thing you'll want to do is hunt for your bike and cycling gear. Identify landmarks near your gear. They will guide you directly to your bike during the race.

If the swim is in open water (rather than a pool), spend some time in the water to get accustomed to the temperature. If you train in a pool, open-water temperature is likely to be much cooler than you're used to. Also, get a feel for the waves and check how quickly the beach drops off into the water. An extremely steep drop-off can provide an unwelcome shock at the start of your race.

The Swim

Depending upon the size of the event and the popularity of triathlons in your area, the number of race participants may vary from a few

Race Tip

Find out what kind of energy drink the race organizers are providing (if any) and use it during your training. This will eliminate any surprise reactions your body may have to the ingredients.

dozen to hundreds. Whether the crowd is big or small, you'll soon discover that during competition the most significant difference between training and competing is that you are surrounded by other people. During the swim, large numbers of people in the water seem intimidating, and it is likely that someone may run into you.

If the field is quite large, race organizers will begin the event in groups, or waves, that may be divided by gender, age group, and, in some cases, professional status. You may be required to wear a color-coded swim cap; the color indicates your starting group. Be prepared for quite a bit of bumping and kicking in the water due to the crowd.

If you are concerned about your safety in the water, put on your swim cap after your goggles. The cap will hold the straps of the goggles in place and guard against jarring. You might also position yourself toward the rear or the side of the swim group in order to avoid contact.

The Ride

The ride really begins in the transition area following the swim. Make sure your helmet is fastened before taking your bike from the

Ironman triathletes wait for the start of the swimming portion of the race. Some will get entangled when everyone hits the water.

rack. Then walk or run your bicycle out of the transition area. In many events it is a safety violation to ride your bike in this zone.

By now the crowds that began the race have started to thin out. The cycling portion of the event should feel very similar to your training rides. When you do encounter another cyclist on the course, give him or her plenty of room. Due to safety concerns, drafting is not allowed during the race. If you have the energy to pass another rider, leave enough room between you and the other cyclist. Make sure you've cleared the other competitor's front tire before pulling in front of him or her.

Ironman competitors are expected to give each other room during the cycling leg of the race.

Drink more fluids than you normally would during a training ride. Whether you realize it or not, the swim dehydrated you somewhat and you still have a long way to go. Also, due to the adrenaline you're feeling, you may be pushing yourself harder than you would in a workout session. This is another good reason to hit the water bottle. And, remember to check your heart rate periodically and pace yourself accordingly. You want to perform at 80–90 percent of your max throughout the triathlon.

The Run

This will be far and away the most difficult run of your life. Focus on the fact that the majority of the race is behind you and that the end is within reach. Begin your run with a slow and steady pace. It may take a while, but you'll soon feel closer to your old self again and you can monitor your performance as if it were a training run. Increase your pace as you feel comfortable doing so.

You can't drink enough fluids during the running leg of your first triathlon. Volunteers will be on hand to provide drinks along the course—grab one at each station. You don't need to finish the entire drink, but you should take a sip or two. This will keep your fluid intake even.

After the Race

Congratulations are in order! Hopefully you finished the event with enough energy to enjoy your personal victory. Keep your feet moving

Subaru Ironman Canada

Held in Penticton, British Columbia, Ironman Canada is the oldest Ironman race held in continental North America. Ironman Canada is also perhaps the most popular Ironman race in history—the 2000 event filled up in one day. Ironman world champions Lori Bowden and Peter Reid, who also happen to be husband and wife, claimed the 2000 Subaru Ironman titles.

It is not uncommon for an athlete to collapse at the end of an Ironman triathlon.

until your heart rate and breathing return to normal levels. A brief cooldown exercise is a good idea when you feel ready. Follow the cooldown with some well-deserved stretching.

Take this time to assess your body's condition. Feel, massage, and appreciate your muscles. Evaluate your performance. Think about how adjustments in your training routine might improve your next event. Think about your future goals. For many, the completion of their first triathlon is really a starting point. It is their first step on the road to Kona and the Ironman!

Progressing from average human to triathlete in three months is a fantastic feat. If you're interested in continuing with the sport, you still have plenty of room in which to grow. Think about improving in terms of endurance, speed, or strength.

The need for speed drives many triathletes. They want to go faster—to race the clock and shave off another few minutes with each event. This is the one constant against which you can measure yourself and your improvement. There are other ways to gauge your progress as a triathlete.

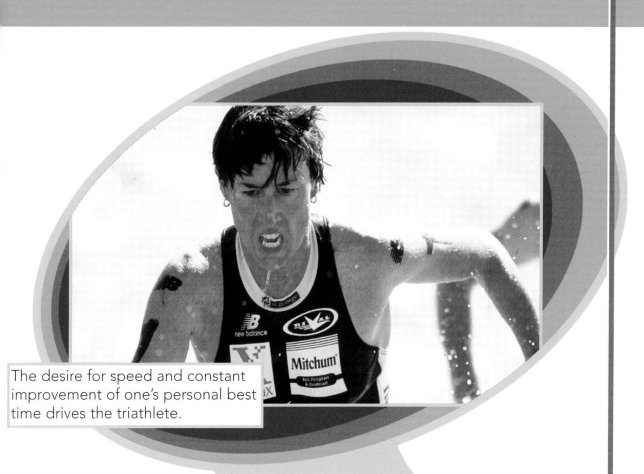

The desire for speed and constant improvement of one's personal best time drives the triathlete.

The First Year

During your first year as an active triathlete, try to add more sprint triathlons to your training calendar. Focus on gaining experience and improving your performance. Your body can endure events every six weeks. You should maintain a workout program that allows for periods of rest and recovery before and after each race.

As you prepare for your second triathlon, write down the times you posted in each sport during the first race. Reduce those times by 5 percent to calculate target times for the next race. Increase the

Finishing any triathlon—sprint, half, or full—gives an athlete a feeling of great accomplishment.

intensity of your training until you can complete race-length workouts within your new target times. On race day, try to complete each sport within your target times. If you achieve this goal, repeat this exercise for your third triathlon—you'll see significant improvements in speed over the course of just a few events.

After completing your third triathlon, you should begin to feel more energetic at the end of the race and confident about your finishing time. For your next goal, add a competitive element to the race. Set objectives within the race, such as passing the person just ahead of you or trying to place one position higher in your age group than you did in your previous race.

The key benefit you'll gain from your first year of competing in triathlons is meeting and talking with other triathletes. You will forge friendships with some extraordinary people. You will also gain access to the best triathlon training information available—personal experience.

An Ironman

Some triathlon training experts believe that a beginning triathlete who is interested in competing at the Ironman level needs eight to ten months to prepare. Of course, an incredibly demanding training program will occupy most of your time during those months. Becoming an Ironman requires genuine commitment.

Since you're about to make a large time investment in this sport, this is a good time to increase your investment in equipment as well. If you haven't already, upgrade your bike to a road-racing model, paying special attention to finding the right frame for your body. You may ride more miles than ever before this year. You owe it to yourself to be safe and comfortable.

Professional triathletes spend up to twenty hours training every week, but you should be able to get into Ironman shape in as little as thirteen hours per week. Still, this leaves less time for social activities, so make your Ironman training a social activity in itself. Train with your friends and have fun!

In preparation for the Ironman, build upon your current triathlon training program. Increase the distance and time of your workouts by 5 percent each week. You should make time for three swimming workouts per week and four each for the ride and the run. It is also important to work a recovery week into your training every fourth or fifth week to give your body a chance to repair and nourish itself.

Peter Reid of Victoria, Canada, wins the Ironman triathlon in Kona, Hawaii, on October 14, 2000.

You need not hang up your equipment for a week during a recovery period. Simply reduce your training in each sport by 50 percent.

Finding an Ironman

Imagine that a year has passed. You stuck with your training program, and you're confident you can complete an Ironman. How do you get into an event?

The World Triathlon Corporation (WTC) hosts twenty-one Ironman triathlons around the world each year and the Ironman World Championship at Kona. Seventeen of these events are full

Ironman-distance triathlons and the other four are half Ironmans. You are eligible to sign up for any Ironman regardless of location, but entry requirements vary from event to event. In order to keep the number of participants at a level that is safe for competitors and manageable for race officials, a limited number of entries are accepted. Check the Ultra Info section at the back of this book for a complete listing of Ironman-sanctioned events and contact information.

Qualifying for Kona

The Ironman World Championship in Kona, Hawaii, is open to any pro or age grouper triathlete who can complete the Ironman distance. For many triathletes, it represents the ultimate challenge.

There are two ways to qualify for one of Kona's 1,500 coveted starting slots. You can earn a qualifying position at an Ironman-sanctioned qualifying race, or complete any half Ironman or Ironman triathlon, and then enter a lottery for a chance at a random slot selection.

A specified number of Kona slots are awarded following each qualifying race. A small percentage are reserved for pros, and the rest are distributed to the best performing age groupers. The top finishing male and female in each age group category earn qualifying slots. The remaining slots are distributed to the best finishers in other races. For those triathletes who completed but did not qualify, the WTC runs two lotteries each year: an American lottery, which grants 150 Kona slots to American citizens, and an international lottery, which grants 50 slots to citizens of other countries. With this system in place, Kona welcomes the best of the

Ironman triathletes find great satisfaction in participating in one of the most challenging athletic competitions around.

best alongside wide-eyed amateurs for an electrifying World Championship unlike any other in professional sports.

If you have the desire to confront the limitations of your body and mind and break through those limits, then you have what it takes to become an Ironman triathlete. If you have a dream to someday compete at Kona, hold onto that dream and work hard to achieve it. In the meantime, take advantage of the everyday benefits of triathlon—bask in the time you spend in wide-open spaces, revel in your friendships, and enjoy the power and strength that comes with being one of the world's most fit athletes.

Glossary

age grouper Amateur triathletes are categorized into groups based on their ages and are referred to as age groupers.

drafting Riding closely behind the cyclist in front of you in order to take advantage of the reduced wind resistance and gain a competitive edge.

duathlon Duathlon is a multisport that combines two individual sports, usually running and cycling.

hypothermia Hypothermia occurs when a person's body temperature drops below 96 degrees Fahrenheit. Symptoms include fatigue, weakness, shallow breathing, confusion, and drowsiness.

multisport A multisport is any sport that combines two or more individual sports. Duathlon and triathlon are examples of multisports.

open-water In triathlon, open water is a body of water that is not a swimming pool. Open-water swims usually take place in the ocean or a lake.

spinning Spinning is an exercise program that utilizes a specially designed stationary bicycle and a series of cycling movements that provide the participant with both a physical and mental workout.

sports drink or **energy drink** Sports and energy drinks are beverages that are rich in nutrients such as sodium and potassium. These drinks are developed to replenish the body's electrolytes lost during rigorous activity.

transition In a triathlon, the transition is the stage in the event when a triathlete prepares for the next sport, following completion of the previous sport.

transition area The specified area where triathletes prepare for the next sport. The gear a triathlete requires for the next sport is stored in the transition area.

triathlete An athlete that participates in triathlons.

triathlon A multisport event that combines three individual sports, usually swimming, cycling, and running.

ultra sport An ultra sport is any sport that is characterized by extreme endurance. Marathons and Ironman triathlons are examples of ultra sports.

In the United States

Blackwater Eagleman Triathlon
6662 Windsor Court
Columbia, MD 21044
Web site: http://www.tricolumbia.org/eagleman.htm

Buffalo Springs Lake Triathlon
P.O. Box 93726
Lubbock, TX 79493
(806) 796-8213
Web site: http://www.buffalospringslaketriathlon.com

Ironman USA Lake Placid Triathlon
Ironman North America
P.O. Box 15207
Panama City, FL 32406
Web site: http://www.ironmanusa.com

Ironman Utah Triathlon
Ironman North America
P.O. Box 15207
Panama City, FL 32406
Web site: http://www.ironmanutah.com

Ironman Wisconsin Triathlon
Ironman North America
P.O. Box 15207
Panama City, FL 32406
Web site: http://www.ironmanwisconsin.com

Janus Ironman Florida Triathlon
Ironman North America
P.O. Box 15207
Panama City, FL 32406
Web site: http://www.ironmanflorida.com

Keauhou Kona Triathlon
P.O. Box 2153
Kailua-Kona, HI 96745
Web site: http://www.keauhoutriathlon.com

Vineman Triathlon
P.O. Box 6007
Santa Rosa, CA 95406
(707) 528-1630
Web site: http://www.vineman.com

In Canada

Subaru Ironman Canada Triathlon
Ironman Canada Race Society
#104 197 Warren Avenue East
Penticton, B.C. Canada V2A 8N8
Web site: http://www.ironman.ca

International

Floripa Brazil Ironman Triathlon
N. A. Promocoes
Rua Fernao Dias
42 santos – SP Brazil 11055-220
Web site: http://www.ironmanbrazil.com

Half Ironman St. Croix
P.O. Box 3955
Christiansted, USVI 00822
Web site: http://www.stcroixtriathlon.com

Half Ironman UK Triathlon
BIG Triathlon Ltd.
41b High Street
Llanberis, Gwynedd LL55 4EU
Wales, U.K.
Web site: http://www.bigtriathlon.com

Ironman Asia Triathlon
6F Hanjoongang Building
IMG Korea
646-7 Yoeksam-Dong, Kangnam-Ku
Seoul 135-080, Korea
Web site: http://www.ironmanasia.com

Ironman Japan Triathlon
Moto-Akasaka Kikutei Building
IMG Tokyo
1-7-18 Moto-Akasaka, Minato-Ku
Tokyo 107-0051 Japan
Web site: http://www.ironmanjapan.com

Ironman Malaysia Triathlon
1st Floor, Wisma Sarma
16 & 18 Jalan Yap Ah Shak
53300 Kuala Lumpur, Malaysia
Web site: http://www.ironmanlangkawi.com.my

Ironman New Zealand Triathlon
P.O. Box 74 447
Market Road
Auckland, New Zealand
+0064 9 522 5346
Web site: http://www.ironman.co.nz

Ironman Switzerland
BK Sportpromotion GmbH
Wattstrasse 5
CH-8307 Effretikon, Switzerland
+41 52 355 1000
Web site: http://www.ironman.ch

Isuzu Ironman South Africa Triathlon
P.O. Box 782674
Sandton, 2146
South Africa
+27 11 807 1486
Web site: http://www.ironmanafrica.com

Kärnten Ironman Austria Triathlon
Triangle Show & Sports Promotion
Paradeisergasse 5
A-9020 Klagenfurt, Austria
Web site: http://www.happynet.at/ironman

Lanzarote Ironman Canarias Triathlon
Club La Santa Events Office
35560 Tinajo, Lanzarote
Canary Islands, Spain
Web site: http://www.ironmanlanzarote.com

Minolta Ironman Australian Triathlon
P.O. Box 153
Tuncurry, Australia
NSW 2428
Web site: http://www.ironmanoz.com

Quelle Ironman Europe Triathlon
Freizeit & Sport Promotion GmbH
Allemannenstrasse 5
D-91174 Spalt
Germany
+49 91 75 9600
Web site: http://www.quelle.ironman.de

Ultra Reading

Allen, Mark, and Bob Babbitt. *Mark Allen's Total Triathlete*. Lincolnwood, IL: NTC Publishing Group, 1988.

Bernhardt, Gale. *Training Plans for Multisport Athletes*. Boulder, CO: Velo Press, 2000.

Crutcher, Chris. *Ironman: A Novel*. New York: Greenwillow Books, 1995.

Friel, Joe. *The Triathlete's Training Bible*. Boulder, CO: Velo Press, 1998.

Kearns, Brad. *Can You Make a Living Doing That?* Palo Alto, CA: Trimarket, 1996.

Mora, John M. *Triathlon 101: Essentials for Multisport Success*. Champaign, IL: Human Kinetics Publishers, 1999.

Plant, Mike. *Going the Distance*. Chicago, IL: Contemporary Books, 1987.

Plant, Mike. *Iron Will: The Triathlete's Ultimate Challenge*. Boulder, CO: Velo Press, 1999.

Thom, Kara Douglass. *Becoming an Ironman*. Halcottsville, NY: Breakaway Books, 2001.

Tinley, Scott. *Triathlon: A Personal History*. Boulder, CO: Velo Press, 1999.

Tinley, Scott, and Mike Plant. *Scott Tinley's Winning Triathlon*. Chicago, IL: Contemporary Books, 1986.

Town, Glenn, and Todd Kearney. *Swim, Bike, Run*. Chicago: Human Kinetics Publishers, 1994.

Online Publications

Xtri.com
http://www.extremetri.com

Inside Triathlon.com
http://www.insidetri.com

Triathlete Magazine
http://www.triathletemag.com

Index

Credits

About the Author

Bill Scheppler has never competed in a triathlon, but he rides his bike to work every day, and we think that's pretty special. A freelance writer specializing in the Internet and interactive entertainment fields, Bill is not afraid to go "lo-tech" every once in a while; after all, he lives in California, where an active lifestyle is required by law.

Photo Credits

Cover, pp. 2, 6, 11, 12, 20, 30, 31, 34, 36, 39, 46 © Robert Beck/Icon SMI; pp. 9, 14 © AP/Wide World Photos; pp. 16, 45 © Sport the Library/Icon SMI; p. 18 © Tim Pannell/Corbis; p. 23 © Jamie Squire/Allsport by Getty Images; p. 26 © Aaron Horowitz/Corbis; p. 28 © Nigel Snowden/STL/Icon SMI; p. 29 © James Davis/ International Stock; p. 40 © Gary Newkirk/Allsport by Getty Images; pp. 5, 42, 44 © Tom Putt/STL/Icon SMI; p.48 © AFP/Corbis; p. 50 © Karl Weatherly/Corbis.

Design and Layout

Thomas Forget